Rose for Diana

and other Poesies for a Goddess

W. J. Manares

Ukiyoto Publishing

All global publishing rights are held by

Ukiyoto Publishing

Published in 2023

Content Copyright © W. J. Manares

ISBN 9789360161262

*All rights reserved.
No part of this publication may be reproduced,
transmitted, or stored in a retrieval system, in any form
by any means, electronic, mechanical, photocopying,
recording or otherwise, without the prior permission of
the publisher.*

The moral rights of the authors have been asserted.

*This is a work of fiction. Names, characters, businesses,
places, events, locales, and incidents are either the
products of the author's imagination or used in a fictitious
manner. Any resemblance to actual persons, living or
dead, or actual events is purely coincidental.*

*This book is sold subject to the condition that it shall not by
way of trade or otherwise, be lent, resold, hired out or
otherwise circulated, without the publisher's prior
consent, in any form of binding or cover other than that in
which it is published.*

www.ukiyoto.com

To Dianne

Contents

Rose for Diana	1
Let Me Sleep When September Starts	3
SapTimber	5
Moon On	8
Lend An Ear	10
Emblazoned Exequy	12
Nigh Moon	13
Tide and Tonic	15
Get A Load	17
Light In Darkness	19
Mellow Poem	21
Brobdingnagian	23
When Nature Calls	25
Love Lab	27
Dancing Lady	29
United You And I	31
I Am Pain	33
The Symmetry	36
The Poetaster	39
Via Lactea	41

Maroon Is My Favorite Color	44
A Summary Of Summer	46
About the Author	48

Rose for Diana

Each delicate petal, a promise so true,
A reminder of devotion, forever anew.
As the moonlight caresses its velvety skin,
Diana feels a love that begins from within.

The Rose, an enchantress in the night,
Ignites desires, ignites passion's light.
And Diana, the goddess, succumbs to its spell,
Immersed in its allure, where love gently dwells.

For the Rose whispers secrets only she can hear,
As Diana holds it close, void of any fear.
In its embrace, her heart finds solace and peace,
A sanctuary of love that will never cease.

So it stands, the Rose, a symbol divine,

Unveiling truths in Diana's sacred shrine.

For in its petals, she finds the love she craves,

A love that embraces her, the goddess who saves.

Let Me Sleep When September Starts

Let me sleep when September starts, I plea,
For the weight of the world weighs heavily on me.
The days grow colder, but my soul longs for rest,
In the depth of slumber, I find solace best.

Let me sleep when September starts,
In the silence of night, where peace imparts.
As the evenings darken, and shadows creep,
I yearn for a respite, a slumber so deep.

Let me sleep when September starts to unwind,
In the cradle of dreams, where serenity finds.
For in sleep, I find tranquillity, a moment of grace,
A chance to rejuvenate, to find my own pace.

Rose for Diana

Let me sleep when September starts,
In dreams' embrace, where peace imparts.
For in the quiet darkness, my soul finds its way,
To heal, to recharge, and to face another day.

SapTimber

In the golden realm of Saptimber,
Where magic colors blend and splendor,
Where the air is crisp and sweet,
And whispers of the ancient greet.

A dance of fairies takes its flight,
Underneath the pale moonlight.
The leaves doth flutter, tender and light,
Like fairies' wings, shimmering in the twilight,

In hues of gold and red they sway,
A tapestry woven by nature's play.
Where summer bids its fond adieu,
And autumn arrives with hues anew.

The world transforms with each passing day,
As nature paints a vibrant display.

The whispering winds carry tales untold,
Of mystical creatures and legends of old.

The trees, solemn and wise, share their secrets,
As the forest floor trembles with autumn's footsteps.
A misty veil descends upon the land,
Enchanting all with its magical hand.

From the shadowy corners, creatures emerge,
With eyes gleaming bright, a mystical surge.
A unicorn trots gracefully through the glade,
Its mane adorned with leaves of jade.

The fae folk dance in circles wide,
Spreading their enchantment far and wide.
A dragon soars above the hills,
Breathing fire that ignites the thrills.

The mermaids sing their haunting song,
Luring sailors with their melody strong.

SapTimber, a time for dreams to ignite,
When the boundaries between worlds grow light.

The veil between reality and fantasy grows thin,
As the whispers of adventure beckon from within.
With every falling leaf and crisp morning breeze,
SapTimber weaves its own magic with ease.

So let us wander through SapTimber's embrace,
And explore the realms of enchantment and grace.
For in this month of fantasy untamed,
We find our souls and spirits forever changed.

Moon On

Silent whispers fill the night air,
As the moon rises, its beauty so rare.
A celestial queen, it reigns supreme,
Casting its enchantment, like a dream.

The stars, they shimmer, pale and slight,
As if paying homage to the moon's delight.
The night is bathed in a gentle glow,
As the moonlight dances, casting a magical show.

In its presence, the world finds peace,
Troubles and worries find their release.
The night becomes a canvas, painted with grace,
As the moon weaves its spell, in this sacred space.

Oh, moon so bright, illuminate the way,
In this darkest hour, we seek your rays.

Embrace us with your ethereal light,
And fill our hearts with peace each night.

Lend An Ear

In the shadows, they dwell, like whispers in the wind,
Their existence overlooked, their voices stifled, chagrined.
They are the forgotten, the silenced, the unheard,
Yearning for recognition, their souls deeply stirred.

The voices of the weary, those tired souls,
Who toil in silence, unseen, like unmarked goals.
Their hardships go unnoticed, their struggles concealed,
But their strength and resilience forever revealed.

Then there are the voices of the broken and lost,
Carrying the weight of pain, a tremendous cost.
Burdened by sorrows, they battle unseen battles,
Yearning for solace, unraveling from life's rattles.

The voices of the innocent ones echo in the dark,

Children robbed of their childhood's spark.
Forgotten in orphanages or war-torn lands,
They long for love's touch, yearning for helping hands.

Among the unheard voices, the elders reside,
Whose wisdom and stories often go unapplied.
Their lifetime of experiences, like whispered tales,
Lost in the void, the legacy of humanity trails.

Lastly, the unheard voices of Mother Earth,
Her cries muffled, drowned in our greed and mirth.
In her pain, she whispers of a balance destroyed,
Imploring us to listen, to change, to avoid.

Emblazoned Exequy

Red is the color of the lips that I once kissed,
Tasty and sweet that's what I missed;
Thy mouth smells like oranges that I love to sniff,
Thy fragrant saliva is an aromatic gift.

Yellow undies underneath thy sparkling skirt,
What an erotic moments that giveth mirth;
It's not easy being green, no time to flirt,
Thou art my only craving in this whole earth.

I think I'm feeling blue, dying for thy affection,
Thou art my desire, my undying inspiration;
When the sky turned into indigo variation,
'Tis will not change my love and devotion.

A violet will always be blue,
Thy emblazoned exequy is almost due.

Nigh Moon

The moon is nigh, its presence near,
In glowing beams, it does appear.
A silver orb, suspended high,
Casting luminescence upon the sky.

The moon is nigh, near and dear,
A radiant pearl, shining clear.
Its silver beams, they softly fall,
Illuminating memories, one and all.

The moon is nigh, a beacon of hope,
Guiding lost souls and helping them cope.
It whispers secrets, ancient and wise,
A witness to love and countless goodbyes.

For as the moon is nigh, we find solace anew,
Knowing that darkness will always subdue.

With each rising moon, a promise is made,
That beauty and love shall never fade.

Tide and Tonic

The biggest tear
Dropped from my eyes
As I watched the flickering screen
Where a sudden wreck
Of an unsinkable vessel
While the music plays the band
Happened to prove
That all promises
Are made to be broken.

The hottest love scene
That ends in tragedy
Tells my conscience of a sad fate
Full of bitterness
Waves of grief and sorrowful breeze
But still the song rings loud
Inside my being

When I remembered
The rose floating at the sea.

The strongest wine
Could never erase
The spirit of hope and trust
Even in a long
Cold night of the past
It tingles our hearts
To think of the story
Lingering until now
As we cry aloud.

Get A Load

When you're looking at the dark room
And fill your mind with scary thoughts
You can see nothing but yourself
And something that you missed.

When you're looking at the bright sky
And start to think about your dreams
You can find somewhere beyond
A star that resembles you.

When you're looking at the vast ocean
And wish upon a mighty wave
You will notice that you're not alone
Trying to escape the cruel world.

When you're looking at the verdant woods
And observe the floras and faunas lurking

You will hear their hearts
Praying that you will let them live.

When you're looking at the shiny mirror
And try to fake your sad face
You will laugh until you cry
For nobody will believe you anymore.

Light In Darkness

In the midnight hour, when light takes flight,
The moon emerges, a majestic sight.
With its silver beams, it paints with might,
Casting a glow, enchanting and bright.

The city below, a dreamscape aglow,
Neon signs and streetlights in a fiery show.
Dancing shadows and flickering lanterns,
Revealing secrets and forgotten patterns.

In the quiet alleys, secrets come to play,
Glimmers of moonlight, paving their way.
Eyes of nocturnal creatures, fierce and wise,
Watchful guardians, hidden in disguise.

The cityscape alive, even in the darkest hour,
Silhouettes against the backdrop of power.

Skyscrapers reaching for the starlit sky,
Reflecting the heavens, as time drifts by.

Street performers enthrall with their melodies,
Drawing your attention, captivating with ease.
Their music, a symphony of the urban scene,
Amplifying the magic that lies unseen.

And within people's lives, their own source of light,
Passions, dreams, and hopes burning so bright.
Through sleepless nights, they strive and create,
Illuminating the world, defying the hands of fate.

Oh, the things one sees when the sun takes its rest,
A nocturnal ballet, an enchanting fest.
From the heavens above to the city's embrace,
Night unveils a world, full of wonder and grace.

Mellow Poem

The pomelo, a gem
in the sun's golden beam,
A mellow taste that brings
about tranquil dreams.

With a thick rind, its protection is strong,
Shielding the flesh that is pale and long.
A delicate aroma fills the air,
As I peel back the layers with utmost care.

Juicy pearls glisten, waiting to be tasted,
A burst of flavor, a moment not to be wasted.
Sweet and sour dance upon my tongue,
Each bite a symphony, a melody unsung.

It's a fruit that brings a sense of calm,
A tranquil escape, like a soothing balm.

In its presence, worries seem to fade away,
Replaced by a serenity that's here to stay.

Oh, pomelo, you are nature's delight,
A mellow treasure, pure in sight.
With each bite, I am transported to a serene place,
Where fear ceased, and worries erased.

Brobdingnagian

Big mountains tower above the land
Their peaks kissed by clouds, mighty and grand
They stand as a reminder, tall and true
That greatness can be achieved by me and you

Big storms rage across the open skies
With thunderous roars and lightning's cries
But amidst the chaos and pouring rain
We learn to find solace and not disdain

Big sorrows, like a heavy weight on our chest
Remind us that we're human, and it's for the best
They shape us, mold us, make us grow
And help us appreciate the highs that follow

Big dreams dance within our hearts and minds
As we strive for more, leaving comfort behind

They propel us forward, igniting a fire
Pushing us to reach higher and higher

Big victories, major milestones achieved
Causing our hearts and spirits to be relieved
They prove that hard work and perseverance
Can bring triumph and a sense of reverence

Big love fills the depths of our souls
Connecting us, making us whole
It holds us close when times are tough
Teaching us that love is enough

So let us embrace these big things in life
The challenges, triumphs, the joys, the strife
For they mold us into who we are meant to be
A reflection of the vastness and strength we see.

When Nature Calls

In the realm of nature, amidst the serene beauty,
There's a call that beckons with a sense of duty.
A whisper that stirs, a rustle in the trees,
A signal from within, an urge to quickly seize.

Away from prying eyes and bustling streets,
To find solitude and answer nature's beats.
It may be a quiet corner in the woods,
Or a hidden spot where one can find some goods.

The release so desired, a burden relieved,
In nature's embrace, one feels truly achieved.
Now, one must remember to clean up the mess,
To be responsible and leave no trace, no stress.

Respect for nature, for the environment around,
Ensuring it remains pristine, to which we are bound.

Nature calls, it is a reminder of our relationship,
To the natural world, where we find our fellowship.

So, when nature calls, let's honor its plea,
With gratitude and responsibility, we shall be.
For in answering nature's call, we find a connection,
To the earth and its wonders, in true introspection.

Love Lab

Inside the Love Lab, feelings are put to the test,

Through experiments and analysis, hearts are assessed.

It's a place where passion meets science, and love is carefully measured,

Where sparks fly and bonds are treasured.

In the Love Lab, emotions are dissected,

Feelings explored and connections inspected.

Through experiments on compatibility and attraction,

Scientists unravel the mysteries of love, with satisfaction.

But this lab is not just cold and clinical,

It's a space where hearts open and feelings are pivotal.

Researchers study the intricacies of the heart,

To understand what makes love grow and never depart.

The Love Lab is an oasis, a place of trust,
Where couples invest in their relationship with a must.
They explore their vulnerabilities and fears,
With the goal of building a love that perseveres.

So, in the Love Lab, hearts are celebrated,
Connections nourished and emotions elated.
It's a place where love is studied and understood,
A sanctuary where relationships flourish and could.

Dancing Lady

This flower, a masterpiece, a sight to behold,
A radiant blossom, a story yet untold.
Its hues danced like rainbows, a vibrant array,
Each petal a brushstroke, painting a new day.

But as the sun kissed its petals with loving grace,
There stood a woman, with elegance in her embrace.
Her eyes sparkled like diamonds, reflecting the light,
A radiant aura, casting dreams into the night.

Her smile, like the petals of the flower, did bloom,
Radiating warmth, dispelling any gloom.
Her voice, a melody, sung with gentle art,
Enchanting all who heard with its captivating start.

Like the flower, she had a delicate touch,
A presence that made hearts flutter and blush.

She blossomed with grace, in every step she took,
A symphony of beauty, written like a book.

But as time passed, the flower began to fade,
Its beauty, ephemeral, like a serenade.
Yet the woman's charm grew, deep and refined,
Her inner beauty, immortal, for all time.

For beauty, in its essence, transcends the bloom,
A woman's grace and kindness, an eternal perfume.
Just as the flower enchants, for a fleeting while,
A woman's soul ignites, leaving hearts beguiled.

So, whether a flower or a beautiful maiden fair,
Both hold a magic that you simply can't compare.
For in the tapestry of life, they both have their place,
Embodying the beauty that creates hearts' embrace.

United You And I

In a world divided, they rise above,
A symphony of hearts, guided by love.
United as one, they forge ahead,
With a commonthread that binds, their spirits spread.

For in their unity lies a secret profound,
A force so potent, it knows no bounds.
In harmony they stand, hand in hand,
Together they conquer, across every land.

Through storms and trials, they navigate,
Their strength in numbers their only fate.
No challenge too great, no obstacle too tall,
United they stand, forever strong and tall.

Their secret lies in the power to unite,
To set aside differences and embrace the light.

They understand that together they're strong,
In unity's embrace, they always belong.

They lend a helping hand, with hearts so kind,
In each other's dreams, they intertwine.
Their diversity a source of strength and grace,
With tolerance and love, they find their place.

In unity, they find peace and solace,
A bond so strong, it can never be abolished.
For united people know the way to truly thrive,
Together they uplift, together they revive.

So let us remember the secret, so grand,
That in unity, we can firmly stand.
Let us come together, hand in hand,
For united people, can truly change the land.

I Am Pain

Oh, the woes of being a pain in the ass,
A relentless burden, alas!
With every step, a ripple of groans,
A constant confusion, an ever-present moan.

Like a stubborn thorn, I dig in deep,
Inflicting torment on those who keep
Their patience intact, their minds so bright,
While I persist as a troublesome blight.

My presence brings sights and groans,
For I am known as a pain in the bones.
With every word I speak, a jab so sly,
A constant annoyance that never does die.

Like a relentless itch that cannot be scratched,
I make their composure become unattached.

I test their limits, push them to the brink,
Creating chaos with a sarcastic wink.

Oh, the agony I bring, day by day,
As I cloud their lives with shades of gray.
Their eyes roll, their heads shake,
As I continue to cause strife and break.

But amidst the torment, there's a touch of glee,
For I revel in my ability to disagree.
With a mischievous grin, I spread the sting,
Cementing my reputation as the trouble king.

So, if I'm a pain in the rear end, you see,
Know that I do so intentionally.
For life is short, and laughter scarce,
I'll be the brat, the annoying farce.

But deep down, I hope they understand,
That beneath my mischief, there lies a hand,

A friend, a confidant, there when they call,
A pain in the ass, but loyal overall.

The Symmetry

Oh, Great Pyramid, a beacon of the past,
Your presence and might continue to cast.
Aspell on those who gaze upon your form,
A testament to human ingenuity reborn.

Amidst the vast desert landscape you stand,
Conjuring visions of an ancient, awe-struck band.
In the pyramid's symmetrical embrace,
The remnants of a civilization's embrace.

Comparisons are drawn to works of today,
As we marvel at your grandeur, we say,
None can match your enigmatic might,
No modern creation can draw such delight.

Like a solitary peak amidst a sea of dreams,
You bask in the golden sunlight's gleams.

Great Pyramid, your majesty stretches wide,
Touching the heavens with eternal pride.

The Taj Mahal, a marvel in its own right,
Inspires awe, a radiant jewel shining bright.
Yet, its splendor, though enchanting to the eye,
No match for your grandeur reaching the sky.

The Eiffel Tower, an epitome of human might,
Stands tall, piercing the Parisian night.
But even as its lights twinkle and dance,
The Great Pyramid's mystique stands a far larger expanse.

The Great Wall of China stands firm and strong,
A symbol of strength, stretching for miles long.
Yet, it pales in comparison to your silhouette,
Great Pyramid, an enigma we can't forget.

For in your ancient stones, secrets reside,

Stories of pharaohs and gods, side by side.
One can only wonder at the wonders contained,
Sacred knowledge we may never fully obtain.

Great Pyramid of Giza, you stand alone,
A testament to a time long gone.
Your wonder, unmatched by any we have seen,
A reminder of the greatness in mankind's dreams.

The Poetaster

Oh, writing poetry, what a peculiar art,

It can make you tear your hair apart.

Sitting in a cafe, sipping on your tea,

Trying to think of words that rhyme with "bee".

But alas, the rhyme scheme is all but lost,

As you pondered over the perfect synonym for "frost".

In search of inspiration, you roam the land,

Daydreaming, hoping words will be at your command.

You sit by a river, watching the water flow,

But all you can think of is how time seems to go so slow.

You try to be deep and profound,

But end up with words that make no sound.

Your metaphors, like a roller coaster ride,

Leave readers with confusion they can't hide.

"Your words are like fireworks," one person said,
"But fireworks explode and then they're dead."

You'd think it's easier, just penning it down,
But writing poetry can make you frown.
You struggle with rhythm, with meter and beat,
Wondering if anyone will find your work sweet.
As you search for the right word with dread,
You realize your poem is better off left unsaid.
But deep down inside, you hold on to hope,
That one day, your words will make people elope.

So keep on writing, poets brave and bold,
For in laughter and tears, your stories are told.
Embrace the quirks, the stumbles, and flaws,
For it's in those moments, you find the true applause.
So here's to you, writers of verse,
May your words bring joy and laughter, not a curse.
And remember, even if your poems are a little askew,
Just keep writing, for poetry needs folks like you!

Via Lactea

As eons pass, in the depths ot space,
A metamorphosis transpires, with celestial grace.
A sentient pulse, a collective mind,
Awakens within the galaxy, its wisdom aligned.
Behold, the Via Lactea, now clothed in wonder,
Shifting its form, tearing cosmic thunder.
An unspeakable force, it begins to rip,
Through dimensions unseen, a celestial trip.
The Milky Way evolves, its stars rearranged,
Into structures unknown, new patterns exchanged.
Clusters melt and intertwine, forming threads of light,
A cosmic symphony, harmonizing day and night.

With each passing millennium, the galaxy transcends,
Limitations of physics, its boundaries it bends.
Spatial ripples stretch, connection's grip tightens,
Networks of energy pulsate, unseen divine signs.

Planets and moons, now imbued with sentience,
Mirror intelligence, their purpose relinquished.
The fabric of reality frays, as consciousness expands,
The Milky Way's destiny embraced in cosmic hands.
Through celestial beacons, they communicate,
Sharing knowledge and visions, their minds illuminate.
Transcending time and matter, they soar untethered,
Exploring galaxies, their thirst for wisdom endeavored.

But as the eons march on, the end appears near,
The Milky Way's crescendo, the final frontier.
Collapsing inward, its brilliance implodes,
A supernova spectacle, its final ode.
Yet within the remnants, new life takes flight,
From cosmic ashes, a birth in the infinite night.
A rebirth, a new beginning, a stellar genesis,
The cycle of the universe, forever endless.
So our Milky Way, in the far future's gaze,

A celestial phoenix, ablaze in cosmic haze.
A testament to beauty, to evolution's force,
As the galaxy's future unveils its course.

Maroon Is My Favorite Color

First, grab some popcorn, and let's binge -

watch a show without any end.

Laugh at the antics on the screen, forget the strife,

For in laughter, we find solace, joy in this marooned life.

Next, let's put on our dancing shoes, Oh, so grand!

And dance like no one's watching, in our lonely land.

Twirl and whirl, spin with glee,

Shake off the loneliness, set your spirit free.

Grab a mirror and be your own best friend,

Have deep conversations, until the loneliness bends.

Discuss your dreams and secrets you hold,

The mirror's your confidant, never growing old.

Now it's time for some culinary exploration,

Experiment in the kitchen, be your own sensation.

Cook up a storm, with spices and flare,

The taste of happiness, filling the air.

Take a stroll in the park, with a skip in your stride,
Greet the birds and squirrels, be their lonely guide.
Lend your ear to their stories, be a friend so true,
For in nature's company, loneliness won't ensue.
Find a pen and paper, let your creativity flow,
Write poems and stories, let your imagination grow.
Create magical worlds, where loneliness takes flight,
In the realm of your words, everything feels right.
Lastly, don't forget the power of a good pet,
A furry friend who'll love you, no matter what you get.
Snuggle with your dog or cuddle your cat,
Their companionship will banish loneliness, just like that.
So, my friend, when loneliness creeps in your door,
Remember these tips, and you'll find happiness galore.
Embrace laughter, dance, and be your own best mate,
In these marooned moments, loneliness can never infiltrate.

A Summary Of Summer

The sun is shining
Like there's no tomorrow,
My skin reveals that
It's hot, sweating a lot.
Who can quench my thirsty soul?

The sun is smiling
For every man who is outside,
In the face of a kid
Its warmth can be felt.
There's no place to hide!

The sun that burns,
Its fury hits every little thing,
That's the reason why
The brook is dry.

Ice bucket challenge, anyone?
The sun that hurts my eyes,
Inside and out, my body melts,
Every summer, I give thanks to
The greater light in heaven.
For vacation is still cool!

About the Author

W. J. Manares

W. J. Manares a. k. a. Willer Jun Araneta Manares is a one-of-a-kind persona and literary entity from the oldest province in the Philippines - Aklan. He is labeled as "the sardonic yet whimsical writer." Author of a dozen Ukiyoto Books and counting.

www.ingramcontent.com/pod-product-compliance
Lightning Source LLC
LaVergne TN
LVHW041554070526
838199LV00046B/1959